TRAILBLAZERS
of the MODERN WORLD

JONAS SALK

By Richard Hantula

WORLD ALMANAC® LIBRARY

Please visit our web site at: **www.worldalmanaclibrary.com**
For a free color catalog describing World Almanac® Library's list
of high-quality books and multimedia programs, call 1-800-848-2928 (USA)
or 1-800-387-3178 (Canada). World Almanac® Library's fax: (414) 332-3567.

Library of Congress Cataloging-in-Publication Data

Hantula, Richard.
    Jonas Salk / by Richard Hantula.
      p. cm. — (Trailblazers of the modern world)
    Includes bibliographical references and index.
    Summary: A biography of the scientist and humanitarian who discovered the vaccine for polio,
a disease which crippled many people in the early part of the twentieth century.
    ISBN 0-8368-5100-5 (lib. bdg.)
    ISBN 0-8368-5260-5 (softcover)
    1. Salk, Jonas, 1914-1995. 2. Virologists—United States—Biography—Juvenile literature.
3. Poliomyelitis vaccine—Juvenile literature. [1. Salk, Jonas, 1914-1995. 2. Scientists.
3. Poliomyelitis vaccine.] I. Title. II. Series.
    QR31.S25H36   2003
    610'.92—dc22
    [B]   2003065788

First published in 2004 by
World Almanac® Library
330 West Olive Street, Suite 100
Milwaukee, WI 53212 USA

Project manager: Jonny Brown
Editor: Jim Mezzanotte
Design and page production: Scott M. Krall
Photo research: Diane Laska-Swanke
Indexer: Walter Kronenberg

Photo credits: © AP/Wide World Photos: 41, 43; © Bettmann/CORBIS: 4, 5, 6, 8, 11, 13, 14, 21, 23, 28 bottom, 29, 30,
32, 33, 34, 35, 36, 38, 39 both, 42; © Ron Boardman; Frank Lane Picture Agency/CORBIS: 24; © Ed Clark/Time Life
Pictures/Getty Images: 10; © CORBIS: 16; © Bill Eppridge/Time Life Pictures/Getty Images: 40; © Al Fenn/Time Life
Pictures/Getty Images: cover, 27; © Martha Holmes/Time Life Pictures/Getty Images: 7; © Hulton Archive/Getty
Images: 25, 28 top; © Hulton-Deutsch Collection/CORBIS: 17; March of Dimes Birth Defects Foundation: 15, 18, 20;
© Science VU/CDC/Visuals Unlimited: 26

Printed in the United States of America

1 2 3 4 5 6 7 8 9 08 07 06 05 04

TABLE of CONTENTS

Words that appear in the glossary are printed in **boldface**
type the first time they occur in the text.

CHAPTER 1

SAVING THE CHILDREN

In the first six decades of the twentieth century, summer could be an anxious time for many American families. A disease called polio usually struck in the summer months, and its victims were often children and young adults. Although many cases of polio were mild, the disease sometimes caused crippling paralysis, with the muscles of the body unable to function properly. Some polio sufferers could not walk without crutches and leg braces, and others had to use wheelchairs. The disease could also affect the lungs, and some victims had to be put inside a special machine, called an **iron lung**, that helped them breathe. In some cases, people died from the disease.

Polio can be passed between people, so children were especially at risk during the summer, when they were more likely to be playing together in large groups. In the summer, many nervous parents would not let their children go to beaches, public swimming pools, playgrounds, or any other place where a crowd of people might be expected. Some schools delayed opening in the fall until the "polio season" was over. Fear of the disease reached a peak in 1952, when the United States suffered its worst polio year ever. That year, almost 58,000 new cases were reported, including 21,000 cases that involved paralysis.

By then, however, a hard-working and determined scientist, Jonas Salk, and his team of researchers were developing a new **vaccine** that could prevent a person from contracting polio. In 1954,

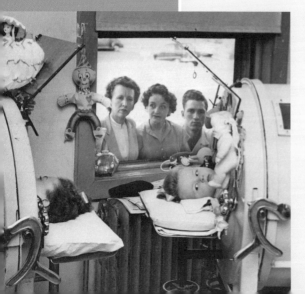

Some polio victims who suffered paralysis had to be kept in iron lungs. These large machines, which left only the head exposed, helped victims breathe.

they began a massive, nationwide **field trial** involving almost two million children—the largest such medical test ever conducted in the United States. The following year, the scientists who conducted the field trial announced that the vaccine was a success. At last, there was a safe and effective vaccine against polio. With this amazing news, the vaccine's creator, Jonas Salk, became a national hero.

Jonas Salk developed the first safe and effective vaccine against polio.

THE POLIO VIRUS

Polio, which is short for poliomyelitis, is caused by a virus. Viruses are **microorganisms** that are even tinier than bacteria. Like certain kinds of bacteria, viruses can be found within other organisms, including humans. Unlike bacteria, viruses exist in a lifeless form when they are outside their "host" organisms, and they are unable to reproduce on their own. But once inside their hosts they are able to reproduce, often causing harm.

The polio virus normally enters through the mouth and travels to the throat and intestines, where it reproduces. It then enters the bloodstream. In most cases, a person infected with the polio virus will have mild symptoms or no symptoms at all. Symptoms can take anywhere from four to thirty-five days to appear, and they may include fever, fatigue, headaches, vomiting, constipation, stiffness in the neck, and pain in the limbs. A person who does not have symptoms can still pass the virus along to other people.

An Ancient Crippler

Historians believe that polio has been around since ancient times. An Egyptian stone tablet, or stele, made about thirty-five hundred years ago, depicts a young man with a withered leg and foot who supports himself with the help of something that resembles a crutch. Historians have suggested the man's leg and foot may have become crippled after he suffered from polio as a child. Descriptions of polio-like symptoms can be found in the ancient writings of the Greek doctor Hippocrates and the Roman doctor Galen. Much later, in 1789, a British doctor, Michael Underwood, made a more precise description of polio, calling it "debility of the lower extremities, [which] . . . usually attacks children previously reduced by fever."

In 1840, the German doctor Jacob von Heine wrote that polio could be contagious. He also suggested it might involve the spinal cord, and he called the disease "spinal infantile paralysis." Well into the twentieth century, infantile paralysis remained a popular name for polio.

This ancient Egyptian stone tablet depicts a man whose right leg is withered, possibly from polio.

If the virus attacks the central nervous system and paralysis occurs, the paralysis develops quickly. The virus destroys the nerves that control muscles, leaving the muscles unable to function. (In the past, a common name for the disease was infantile paralysis.) Polio usually affects the legs more than the arms, but it can also impair a person's ability to swallow, speak, or breathe. Many polio victims who suffer paralysis eventually recover some use of their muscles. In later years, however, they may experience fatigue, pain in their joints and muscles, and an increasing lack of muscle strength.

After the polio vaccination was introduced, polio almost completely disappeared in countries in North and South America, Europe, and Oceania. Polio cases still occur in other parts of the globe, especially in countries in Asia and Africa, but health officials are working to make the world free of the disease, and the number of new cases reported worldwide is now very small. Today, most people have no idea that polio once inspired widespread fear, or that this devastating, unpredictable disease affected thousands of lives every year.

MODERN EPIDEMIC

Polio has been around for thousands of years, but it became a more widespread problem at the end of the nineteenth century. At this time, large outbreaks began occurring in industrialized countries such as the United States, with the disease claiming more older victims than in the past. The first known instance of a large outbreak occurred in 1894, when more than 130 cases were reported in Vermont. In 1916, a polio **epidemic** struck the country. New York City reported 9,000 polio cases, with more than 2,300 deaths resulting from the disease, and the nationwide total was 27,000 cases and 6,000 deaths. Health officials did not know how to cope with the mysterious disease, and the public's anxiety about polio continued to grow in the following decades as new outbreaks occurred. Most polio victims who suffered paralysis survived, but they often remained dependent on their braces, crutches, wheelchairs, and iron lungs—visible reminders of the disease's crippling effects.

With his crippled legs in braces, this young polio victim helps raise money for a new hospital in 1948.

For a long time, scientists could not explain why polio had started occurring in large outbreaks, but many came to believe that polio epidemics were actually the result of improved sanitation practices, such as the treatment of drinking water and sewage. Better sanitation had reduced many diseases, but polio presented a special problem.

When people are infected with a polio virus, their **immune systems** develop protective **antibodies** that usually make them resistant (immune) to future infections. In the less sanitary environment of the past, polio viruses were often present, and many people were infected at a very young age. The infection would usually be mild (especially for infants, who received antibodies against polio from their mothers' breast milk), but it would result in protection against future infection. With improved sanitation, however, fewer people were exposed to the polio virus, especially at an early age. But people who were not exposed to polio did not develop immunity against future infections. If they did become infected with polio, either later in childhood or as adults, the disease was likely to be more severe, and their bodies had no protection against it.

By 1908, Karl Landsteiner and Erwin Popper had discovered that polio was caused by a virus. But progress in unraveling the secrets of polio and creating a vaccine was slow in coming. In the first half of the twentieth century, researchers developed many drugs to treat diseases caused by bacteria, but these drugs did not work against the polio virus or any other virus. In the 1930s, scientists tried to produce vaccines to prevent polio, and the vaccines were tested on children.

Karl Landsteiner (below) and Erwin Popper discovered that polio is caused by a virus.

But the vaccines failed, and the tests resulted in several deaths. This disastrous outcome led many researchers to doubt that a polio vaccine was even possible.

Two Vaccines

Today, two different kinds of polio vaccine are available. The first kind, which was developed by Jonas Salk, is made from "killed," or inactivated, polio viruses. These viruses cannot cause infection, but they can still prompt the body to produce antibodies against them. The second kind of vaccine was introduced in the early 1960s and was developed by a scientist named Albert Sabin, who worked to develop a polio vaccine during the same time as Salk. This vaccine uses "live," or active, viruses that have been made very weak. They result in a mild infection, causing the body to produce antibodies, but they are usually too weak to do any harm. The Salk vaccine is delivered with a series of shots. The Sabin vaccine can be taken orally. Both vaccines are effective and have been improved in recent years.

BEATING THE VIRUS

It is not surprising that Salk believed he could create an effective polio vaccine, despite the doubts of many scientists. Salk often stuck to his beliefs when he was sure he was right, even when those beliefs were at odds with the opinions of others. When Salk began the polio vaccine project, for example, he used inactivated polio viruses. A vaccine works by introducing a small amount of a virus into the body, so the body can produce antibodies against it. Vaccines can use "live" (active) viruses, which have been made very weak and cause a small infection, or "killed" (inactive) viruses, which cause no infection at all. Vaccines using live viruses had proven to be very effective, but they were also potentially harmful—some people contracted the very disease the vaccine was sup-

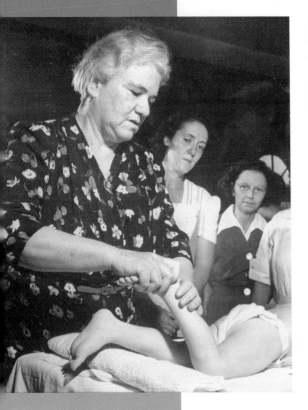

The fight against polio did not only take place in the United States. In this photo, Australian nurse Elizabeth Kenny, a leading expert on physical therapy for polio victims in the 1940s, demonstrates a technique to a group of American nurses.

posed to prevent. Most experts doubted that a vaccine using killed viruses would be effective against polio. But Salk was convinced that he could create such a vaccine, and he ultimately proved the experts wrong.

No matter how many obstacles Salk faced, he always kept working toward his goal. He managed his research team with an able hand, giving instructions or friendly advice as needed. His son Peter, who also became a researcher, once commented, "Sometimes I get the feeling that all the work I might be doing is fruitless. But he always comes along, tells me not to get depressed and suggests another experiment."

The result of Salk's dedication and single-minded determination was a vaccine that nearly eradicated polio in the United States. By 1960 there were only 2,525 reported cases of paralytic polio in the country.

In subsequent years, a vaccine created by another polio researcher, Albert Sabin, was used more widely than Salk's vaccine. The Sabin vaccine is made of live viruses, and although it is generally safe, it can cause infection. Between 1980 and 1998, the United States averaged just eight cases of polio a year, most of which were believed to be due to the Sabin vaccine itself. In the United States today, the Salk vaccine, which never causes polio, is once again preferred for most situations.

A NEW YORK CHILDHOOD

Jonas Edward Salk was born in New York City on October 28, 1914. His parents, both of Russian-Jewish descent, had met while working in the city's garment industry. Salk's father, Daniel, was from New Jersey and designed women's blouses and neckwear. His mother, Dora, also called Dolly, had come to the United States from Russia. She found work in a garment factory but gave up her job when she married Daniel.

The Salk family was not well-off. Daniel did not finish high school, and Dora received little or no formal schooling. The couple wanted their children—Jonas and two younger sons, Lee and Herman—to enjoy a better life, and they encouraged the three to study diligently and become successful. All three brothers eventually went to college and made careers in the health field.

An early-twentieth-century street scene in New York City, where Jonas Salk was born

Jonas did so well in school that he skipped some grades and was accepted into Townsend Harris High School, a special public school in New York for gifted children. It did not offer much science instruction, however, and physics was the only science course Jonas took while he attended the school. When Jonas graduated in 1929, he knew he wanted to help people, and he had thoughts of becoming a lawyer. Many years later Donna Salk, Jonas's wife during the years he developed the polio vaccine, noted, "Jonas had the idea, from a time when he was quite young, that he wanted to do something that would make a difference to humanity."

PAINFUL TIMES

Although Jonas's childhood had been pleasant enough, he recognized that many people faced hardship and suffering. From his parents, he learned that Jews in Russia experienced persecution and were even the victims of violence. He could also see for himself how difficult life was in the poor neighborhoods where his family lived. The day after his fifteenth birthday, on October 29, 1929, the U.S. stock market suffered a disastrous crash. This crash marked the beginning of the **Great Depression**, during which millions of people in the United States lost their jobs, their savings, and their homes.

Jonas grew up during the period of recurring, large-scale outbreaks of polio that began with the great polio epidemic of 1916. He was less than two years old when the 1916 epidemic struck. Most of the epidemic's victims were under the age of five, and Jonas luckily escaped the disease. But New Yorkers long remembered the epidemic, and the frantic efforts to do something, anything, that might help to ease the crisis.

Polio's Horrors

Today, it can be hard to imagine the pain and suffering created by polio epidemics in the first half of the twentieth century. In his biography of Salk, *Breakthrough*, Richard Carter quotes a nurse who worked at Municipal Hospital, where Salk had his laboratory: "In all my career there has been no experience like Municipal Hospital before the Salk vaccine. One year the ambulances literally lined up outside the place.... One of our resident physicians never went to bed for nights on end, except for stretching out on a cot in his clothes. We nurses could never get home on time, either. To leave the place you had to pass a certain number of rooms, and you'd hear a child crying for someone to read his mail to him or for a drink of water or why can't she move, and you couldn't be cruel enough to just pass by. It was an atmosphere of grief, terror, and helpless rage.... I remember a high school boy weeping because he was completely paralyzed and couldn't move a hand to kill himself. I remember paralyzed women giving birth to normal babies in iron lungs...."

Iron lungs are jammed into a Boston hospital room during a polio epidemic in 1955.

City authorities washed the streets with water daily and ordered the killing of thousands of stray cats. Some polio victims and their relatives were **quarantined** and some victims were put in hospitals, where they were not allowed to mix with non-polio patients. Nearby towns tried to bar New Yorkers from entering. Children were not allowed in movie theaters and could not take trains unless they had certificates of good health. For a while, children were not even allowed to enter the New York Public Library. Schools opened a month later than usual.

During a polio outbreak in 1916, health officials posted this sign, which warns people to "keep off this street."

In 1917, the United States entered World War I (1914–1918). The following year, when the war was in its final months, a deadly epidemic of influenza, or "flu," swept over much of the world. Like polio, the disease is caused by a virus, and it resulted in more than twenty million deaths—far more than the total number killed during the war. The number of people killed by influenza in the United States alone ran into the hundreds of thousands.

Two Leaders in the Polio Fight

In the decades before Salk created his vaccine, two powerful men played central roles in raising money for the fight against polio. These men were Franklin Delano Roosevelt and Basil O'Connor.

Roosevelt was president of the United States from 1933 until 1945. He was also probably the most famous polio victim in history. In 1921, Roosevelt was diagnosed with polio. His legs were permanently crippled and he could not walk without assistance. At the time, Roosevelt was thirty-nine years old and had a promising political future with the Democratic Party. For the next few years, however, Roosevelt spent much of his time on treatments that might help him regain control of his legs. In 1924, he visited Warm Springs, Georgia, a dilapidated resort that had naturally warm waters said to be beneficial to sufferers of paralysis. Swimming in the resort's waters failed to cure Roosevelt's paralyzed leg muscles, but it did strengthen other muscles and improve his spirits. In 1926, Roosevelt bought the resort. Later, with O'Connor's help, he turned it into a nonprofit foundation that conducted polio research and helped people suffering from the disease.

O'Connor was a New York Wall Street lawyer by profession. In 1924, he proposed to pay Roosevelt in return for the right to use Roosevelt's name to attract business. The two men worked together well, and when Roosevelt returned to politics a few years later, he left O'Connor in charge of Warm Springs. In the years that followed, O'Connor helped lead the battle against polio. He became good friends with Jonas Salk and lent his powerful support to some of Salk's projects.

Basil O'Connor headed the National Foundation for Infantile Paralysis, which raised money to fight polio. Its "March of Dimes" fund-raising campaigns were highly successful.

This epidemic no doubt made an impression on the young Jonas—as did the effects of the war. Many years later, Salk told an interviewer that he still remembered watching a parade, in 1918, to celebrate the end of World War I. Soldiers who had returned from the war marched in the parade, and many bore obvious signs of their wartime injuries. Salk recalled wanting very much to help the wounded soldiers.

CHAPTER 3

THE MAKING OF A SCIENTIST

Following high school, Salk entered the City College of New York. His plans to go into law didn't last long. One person who was against the idea was Salk's mother. According to Salk, she didn't think he would be very good at law, because, he said, "I really couldn't win an argument with her." Salk was not very interested in science when he was a child, but now chemistry and similar subjects began to intrigue him. He switched to a **pre-med** program, intending to go into research after medical school.

MEDICAL SCHOOL

After graduating from college in 1934, Salk enrolled in the New York University School of Medicine. At the end of his first year, Salk got his first big break when R. Keith Cannan, a chemistry professor, suggested Salk take a year off to work with him in **biochemistry**. Salk now had an opportunity to experience the world of research and to do a little student teaching, and he jumped at the chance.

While in medical school, Salk attended two lectures that would have important implications for his later work with the polio vaccine. The two lectures seemed to represent contradictory views on how a human body could develop immuni-

A chemistry student works on an experiment in the 1930s.

ty to a disease. One lecture involved diseases caused by toxins, or poisonous substances, that were produced by certain bacteria. This lecture made the argument that toxins could be treated with chemicals to make them harmless and then put into the body to stimulate immunity to the diseases. The other lecture discussed immunization against a disease caused by a virus. Reflecting the opinions of most scientists at that time, it made the argument that a person had to actually experience infection to develop immunity. Therefore, a vaccine made from viruses that had been inactivated by chemical treatment would never produce immunity. After attending the two lectures, Salk wondered how inactivating something and putting it in the body could produce immunity in one case, but not the other. This line of thought eventually led him to develop an effective polio vaccine using killed viruses.

President Roosevelt at one of a series of balls held on his birthday during the 1930s to raise money for the fight against polio.

In his last year at New York University, Salk was able to work with Dr. Thomas Francis, Jr., a prominent **epidemiologist** and an expert on influenza and other viruses. Francis was one of the few leading scientists in the United States who believed in the potential of killed-virus vaccines, and he studied whether influenza viruses could be killed with **ultraviolet light** but still provide immunity against the disease. In 1939, Salk graduated from medical school. His internship—the period of practical training in a hospital that usually follows graduation from medical school—was supposed to begin several months later. In the meantime, Salk continued his work with Francis.

Although Salk was a conscientious student who worked hard to prepare himself for his chosen career, he also had a full life outside of school. The day after Salk received his medical degree, he got married to a woman named Donna Lindsay, a social worker. The couple had met one summer at Woods Hole, a town in Massachusetts where she was spending her vacation and he was working in a lab. Salk and his new wife hoped to raise a family.

"A Good Dancer"

Jonas Salk's first wife, Donna, was an attractive and intelligent young woman who had been an honor student at Smith College, where she studied psychology. Donna later recalled that when she met Jonas, he did not at all seem like a person with few interests outside the lab. "He was a good dancer," she said, "an amusing and exciting conversationalist, and as different from the stereotype of the one-track scientist as anyone could possibly be."

TRAINING COMPLETED

Salk's internship—at Mount Sinai Hospital in New York City—was a two-year program that began in March 1940. The competition to become an intern at Mount Sinai was fierce. Only a dozen positions were available, and 250 people applied. Salk's excellent qualifications won him admission. Once there, he continued to excel, earning a reputation among other interns and senior doctors as a talented young physician. He knew how to talk with patients in a warm and pleasant way, he was good at diagnosing their ailments, and he showed a knack for surgery.

The March of Dimes

U.S. president Franklin Roosevelt, who had been diagnosed with polio long before he was elected to office, knew the tragedy of the disease firsthand. In 1938, he established the National Foundation for Infantile Paralysis, with Basil O'Connor as its president. The foundation's purpose was to conduct national campaigns to raise money for polio research, the care of polio patients, education about the disease, and special training for health-care professionals.

Comedian Eddie Cantor suggested asking people to give dimes for the fight against polio.

The foundation's first major campaign used a novel fund-raising method that was based on an idea put forth by Eddie Cantor, a famous comedian at the time. Cantor proposed that national radio shows ask people across the country to send a tiny amount, say a dime, right to the White House. "Think what a thrill the people would get," said Cantor. "And we could call it the March of Dimes!" The name was meant to echo "The March of Time," which was the title of a popular series of **newsreels**.

The results of the campaign were astounding. A flood of mail hit the White House, and it took months to be sorted. That first March of Dimes campaign gathered more than $1,800,000, including 2,680,000 dimes. Americans came to view the foundation as the main organization in the struggle against polio, and its annual campaigns grew more and more successful. Celebrities pitched in to help. In 1946, the foundation began featuring a "poster child"—a single polio victim that it selected each year to help publicize its activities. Regional and local "poster children" were also chosen. By 1955, the foundation's annual revenue had reached $67,000,000.

Following the success of the Salk vaccine in the mid-1950s, the foundation began shifting its focus to birth defects. In 1979, it officially changed its name to the March of Dimes.

As Salk's internship neared its end, he began looking for a research position. He wanted to stay in New York, but Mount Sinai did not usually hire its interns, and he was turned down at other places in the city. Salk may have been rejected because his research experience and his scientific interest—immunity to diseases that were caused by viruses—did not match the needs of the places where he applied. Apparently, however, Salk also met opposition because he was Jewish, and **anti-Semitism** existed among some potential employers.

Salk decided to accept an offer to join Thomas Francis in Ann Arbor, Michigan. Francis had left New York University in 1941 to become head of the Department of Epidemiology at the University of Michigan's School of Public Health. In light of his later work, Salk's decision proved to be an important one.

Retired baseball star Babe Ruth visits young polio patients at a New York hospital in 1941.

CHAPTER 4

A MATTER OF MILITARY IMPORTANCE

In the spring of 1942, Salk and his wife Donna moved to Ann Arbor, Michigan, and he began his new job with Thomas Francis at the University of Michigan. In his first year, Salk earned about $40 a week. This money came from a grant paid by the National Foundation for Infantile Paralysis—a foundation established by U.S. president Franklin Roosevelt, who was a polio victim, to raise money for the fight against the disease—in cooperation with the U.S. National Research Council. Jonas and Donna lived outside the city in an old farmhouse that was equipped with a wood-burning stove. They grew much of their own food in a big vegetable garden they planted. In 1944, the couple's first child, Peter, was born. Three years later they had a second son, Darrell.

A KILLED-VIRUS FLU VACCINE

In addition to his university post, Francis headed the Army Influenza Commission and was in charge of a U.S. effort to develop an effective vaccine against influenza. At the time, World War II (1939–1945) was raging, and the U.S. military had an urgent need for an influenza vaccine. The massive 1918 influenza epidemic, at the end of World War I, had killed more than 40,000 U.S. troops.

Developing influenza vaccines was a tough job. First, there are many different types of influenza viruses, and immunity against one type will not prevent infection by another type. An effective vaccine would have to provide U.S. soldiers with immunity against all the different virus types they were expected to encounter. Second, the U.S. military was reluctant to use live-virus vaccines, because the vaccines did occasionally cause the disease they were supposed to be preventing. Most virus experts at the time, however, believed that live viruses were required to make a fully effective vaccine.

Francis and Salk focused on using killed viruses. By 1943, Francis, with the assistance of Salk, had managed to make and test a killed-virus vaccine that provided a limited defense against some types of influenza. Eventually, millions of U.S. troops received influenza vaccines that had originated in Francis's research program.

While working on the influenza vaccine, Salk devised a way to estimate the levels of antibodies in blood samples. Salk was able to demonstrate that the strength of a person's immunity depended on a high level of antibodies. He also helped Francis show that killed-virus influenza vaccines could produce antibody levels as high as those resulting from an actual flu infection.

Salk spent more than five years at Ann Arbor. Working under Francis, he matured into a skilled, professional scientist. He gained valuable experience in developing and testing vaccines and became an expert on the issues involved in stimulating the body's immune system to protect against influenza. He also learned about the management of large projects, because when Francis was unavailable, he was the acting director of the U.S. Army Influenza Commission. At the end of the war, Salk went to Germany to set up labs for diag-

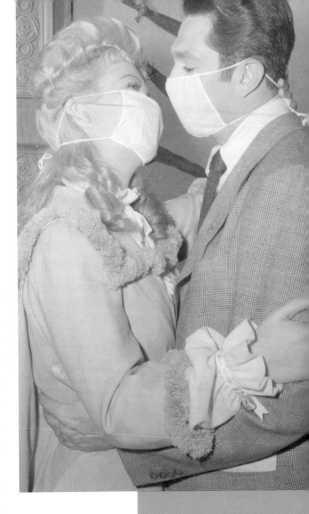

During a 1940s epidemic, Hollywood actors wore masks in rehearsals to guard against transmitting the flu virus.

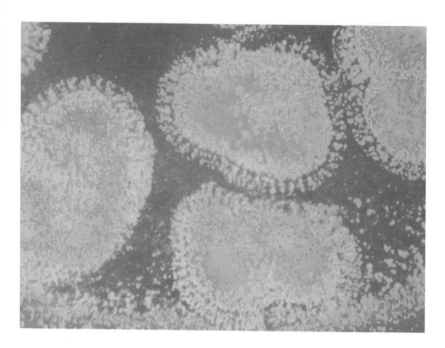

nosing influenza, in case an epidemic should break out. It was an experience, and a responsibility, that he enjoyed immensely.

INDEPENDENCE

By 1946, Salk was ready to leave Thomas Francis and explore his own scientific ideas. "I wanted to do independent work and I wanted to do it my way," he later said. An opportunity to leave came in 1947, when the University of Pittsburgh School of Medicine offered Salk a job and promised to help him build his own virus research program. Salk's friends and colleagues advised him against taking the job. Pittsburgh was known as a dirty industrial town with a severe air pollution problem, and the medical school was of a far lower quality than it is today, with most instructors working only part-time. Very little research was being done, and the school's dean had invited Salk to come in hopes that he would help upgrade its scientific standing. Salk saw the

Top Billing

Jonas Salk was an ambitious man. He badgered Thomas Francis to put his name first in the list of authors in the scientific papers they wrote about their research. Salk knew his career would benefit if he were listed first. His name would be noticed by scientists around the country, because the first spot in the authors list traditionally went either to the research team's leader (in this case, Francis) or to the scientist who played the chief role in the work being reported (which might also be Francis, depending on the research they had performed). Salk told Francis, "Everyone knows who you are. It doesn't matter whether your name is first or last." Francis later reflected, "You couldn't really dislike this in the man, you know. You've got to admire ambition, especially when it's combined with the kind of ability this fellow had." In any case, Salk's name was listed first in several of their publications.

offer as a good opportunity, and he readily accepted. He later commented, "I can remember someone asking me, 'What's in Pittsburgh, for heaven's sake?' and I answered, 'I guess I fell in love.' What I was in love with, of course, was the prospect of independence."

The industrial landscape of Pittsburgh, Pennsylvania, in the 1940s

CHAPTER 5

SEARCH FOR A VACCINE

The Salk family moved to Pittsburgh in 1947, settling in the suburb of Wexford. Their third son, Jonathan, was born three years later.

The university assigned Salk space for his virus research laboratory in the basement of the city hospital, which was located next to the medical school. Although the facilities were not as good as those in Michigan, there was room to expand—which was precisely what Salk's laboratory eventually did.

Salk continued his research on influenza vaccines for the military. After a few months in Pittsburgh, however, the National Foundation for Infantile Paralysis invited him to join a project it was launching to "type" different polio viruses. Salk lacked experience working with polio, but he considered the foundation's offer to be an excellent opportunity. At the very least, he would learn a lot about the polio virus, and there was a chance the foundation might provide more funding in the future. He accepted the offer.

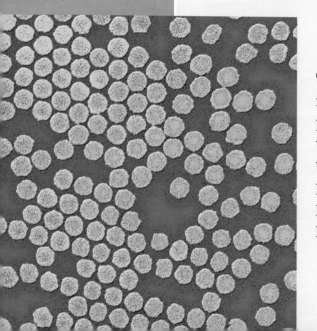

Polio viruses, highly magnified

TYPING POLIO VIRUSES

The purpose of the new project was to find out how many different types of polio viruses existed. Polio presented the same problem as influenza—infection with one type of virus could only prompt the body's immune system to protect against future infections of that particular type, not any other types. In order to make a vaccine that would work against all types of polio viruses, scientists first had to identify all the various types.

In 1948, two research groups reported that, based on a study of a small number of polio virus samples, there were three basic types of polio virus. To find out if any more existed, the foundation planned to have several separate laboratories—including Salk's lab—identify polio virus types in a large number of samples. The project was very complex, and it was intended to last three years.

The polio typing project involved injecting polio viruses into animals and observing the responses of their immune systems. Finding and caring for the animals took a lot of effort, and the project itself required an enormous amount of tedious and repetitive work. The task would have been easier if small animals such as mice could have been used. The researchers had to use monkeys, however, since the only known place where polio virus would readily grow—besides in humans—was the nervous system of monkeys.

Salk devised some shortcuts and finished his part of the foundation's typing project ahead of schedule. The project's final conclusion was that all polio viruses studied belonged to one of the three known types. Researchers could not absolutely rule out the existence of another type. They could, however, go ahead with developing a vaccine, because if a fourth type of virus existed, it was rare.

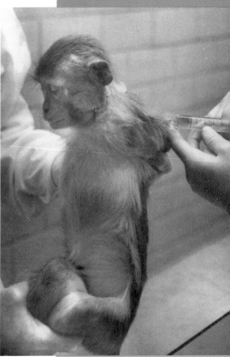

Testing the Salk polio vaccine on a monkey

BREAKTHROUGH

To develop a practical vaccine, researchers had to find a way to obtain large quantities of polio virus, both for

Salk in his lab at the University of Pittsburgh

For their work on the polio virus, Thomas Weller (left), Frederick Robbins (center), and John Enders won a Nobel Prize in 1954.

study and for vaccine production. The need to use monkeys was an obstacle, because the animals were expensive and in limited supply. Attempts to grow the polio virus in test tubes had all failed.

Then, in 1949, Harvard scientist John Enders and his colleagues Thomas Weller and Frederick Robbins reported that they had succeeded in growing the polio virus in test tubes, using tissue from monkey kidneys. This break-through allowed researchers to obtain unlimited amounts of virus, and it also guaranteed a certain level of safety for any potential vaccines. In the past, the polio virus had to be obtained from tissue in a monkey's nervous system, but this tissue could provoke deadly reactions in humans, and researchers were afraid of vaccines being contaminated with it. The breakthrough earned Enders, Weller, and Robbins a Nobel Prize in 1954.

KILLED VIRUS VERSUS LIVE VIRUS

Salk quickly utilized this new breakthrough in his own research, and by 1950 he was ready to begin working on a killed-virus polio vaccine for humans. About the same time—after decades of failure by other scientists—an American virus specialist named Isabel Morgan finally succeeded in making a killed-virus polio vaccine that seemed to work in monkeys. Morgan killed the virus with formalin, a solution of **formaldehyde** that Thomas Francis had also used at Michigan. Critics, however, suggested that Morgan's vaccine may have contained some live viruses, and that even if it did consist only of killed viruses, what worked in monkeys might not work in humans.

Salk also used formalin to kill the polio virus. He worked hard to find the best way to use the solution. It had to inactivate the virus so the vaccine would be safe for people. At the same time, however, the solution could not destroy the virus entirely, because then the virus would not cause the human body's immune system to produce antibodies.

While Salk worked on his killed-virus vaccine, Albert Sabin, at the University of Cincinnati, continued to pursue a vaccine using live but weakened viruses.

At the time, good arguments could be made for and against both approaches. Live-virus vaccines had been around for a long time—the very first successful vaccine, which used live viruses to create immunity against **smallpox**, was introduced in the late eighteenth century. These vaccines also produced long-lasting immunity, and no one knew if immunity induced by a killed-virus vaccine would last as long. Live-virus vaccines offered a bonus benefit— since they used live viruses, they could conceivably spread from a vaccinated person to unvaccinated people, who might then become immune. On the other hand, a killed-virus vaccine might be safer—a live-virus vaccine could potentially change into a more dangerous form

Polio researcher
Albert Sabin

and cause disease. Another advantage of a killed-virus vaccine was the relatively short time needed to develop it, since developing a live-virus vaccine was a much more complex process. The National Foundation for Infantile Paralysis provided funding to both Salk and Sabin.

Single-mindedness

With work on the polio vaccine in high gear, Salk's thoughts tended to focus exclusively on the project. One night he came home from the lab, plopped down in his chair and resumed thinking. His wife Donna tried to talk to him but he did not answer. "You're not even listening to me," she complained. He smiled and said absentmindedly, "My dear, you have my undevoted attention."

Life in his laboratory was hectic. "We worked like dogs," recalled one assistant in Richard Carter's book *Breakthrough*. "It was like a factory, but those of us who knew how unusual that kind of speedup was in a university lab did not mind, because we felt we were part of a closely knit team engaged in a great effort. Jonas was no longer as warm and friendly as he had been in the beginning, but we attributed that to the strain of the work. The bravery he was showing in going ahead so rapidly toward human experiments was also terribly admirable, we felt. So if one of us accomplished something today but accomplished nothing tomorrow and Jonas's attitude seemed to convey a feeling of 'What have you done for me lately?' we took it in good spirit."

Salk checks the work of a lab assistant.

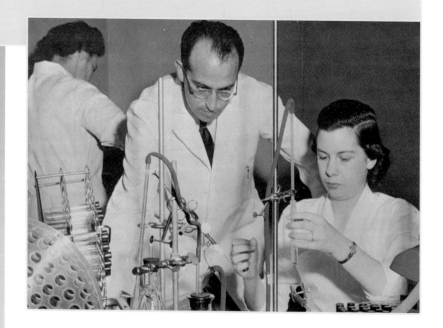

FIRST TESTS IN HUMANS

In the spring of 1952, Salk began testing his killed-virus vaccine on humans. Salk, his family, and his research staff were the first to receive the injections. He then gave shots to residents of the Polk State School in Polk, Pennsylvania, which housed retarded individuals, and to children at the D. T. Watson Home for Crippled Children near Pittsburgh, many of whom had already contracted polio. The vaccine produced no harmful effects, and it caused antibody levels to rise.

Testing Vaccines on Humans

Today, when scientists in the United States develop a new drug or vaccine, they cannot test it on humans without first gaining approval from the U.S. Food and Drug Administration. This government agency has established strict regulations for testing. Before it will approve testing, it considers evidence that the new drug or vaccine is reasonably safe. After the agency grants approval, the initial tests are usually performed on a few people. If the results are promising, researchers may be allowed to test on as many as several thousand people.

When Jonas Salk was developing his polio vaccine, over fifty years ago, medical tests were not so tightly controlled. The government had few official restrictions on testing, and researchers could move on to large-scale tests more quickly than they can today. In fact, the massive 1954 field trial of Salk's vaccine—which involved providing the vaccine to hundreds of thousands of schoolchildren—would probably not be possible today.

Salk understood, however, that any tests he conducted would come under public scrutiny. Despite the desperate need for a vaccine, there was widespread fear of its potential risks, and the memory of previous tests in the 1930s, when deaths had resulted, was still fresh in many people's minds. Likewise, there had previously been an uproar over other, unrelated medical experiments involving federal prisoners, in which some inmates had died. At the time, it was common for medical researchers to carry out small medical trials at institutions, such as prisons or state schools, where groups of people could be easily monitored. But Salk proceeded slowly and with great caution. His testing at the Polk School, for example, began only after Pennsylvania state officials completed a lengthy approval process.

Eleanor Roosevelt, the wife of U.S. president Franklin Roosevelt, with two of her grandchildren. Both children contracted polio but fully recovered. This 1953 photo shows the children making a contribution to the March of Dimes.

Salk did not immediately publicize his results. He wanted to expand the testing program slowly and carefully. As he continued working to improve his experimental vaccine, he was hesitant to test it on large numbers of people before he was sure it was as safe and effective as possible. But 1952 became the worst polio year on record in the United States, and the epidemic was fueling the public's anxiety over the disease. When Salk reported his tests to a meeting of polio specialists in January 1953, some felt the time had come for a large field trial.

WORD SPREADS

Salk wrote a report on his experimental vaccine for the March 28, 1953, issue of the *Journal of the American Medical Association*. At that point, he wanted only to share news of the vaccine with other scientists and doctors, and his report described both what had been accomplished and what remained to be achieved before widespread testing of the vaccine could be considered. He was leery of talking about his work to the popular media. It was accepted practice among scientists to avoid telling the press about new research findings before reporting them in specialized scientific journals. In these journals, scientists disclosed the full details of their work, so other experts could assess their conclusions and catch any mistakes that might have been made. Salk was also afraid that if the general public learned about what he had developed, many people would assume that a safe, effective vaccine would soon be ready.

Word of Salk's work, however, soon leaked to the popular press. "New Polio Vaccine—Big Hopes Seen" was the headline of an article by a popular columnist. Worried that public enthusiasm for his vaccine would get out of hand, Salk decided to make a national radio broadcast to try to set matters straight. He wanted to impress upon the public that his vaccine was experimental, and that even if it someday proved safe and effective enough for general use, time would be needed to develop techniques for producing it in large quantities. Salk's broadcast, on March 26, was headline news, and it angered some researchers. They suspected that Salk's decision to announce his findings in public, before they came out in a scientific journal, was proof that he was really just interested in the spotlight.

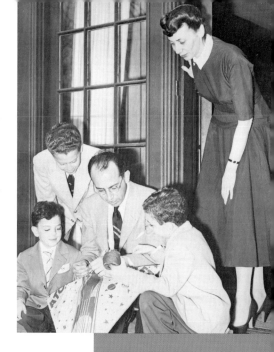

Salk enjoys a moment of relaxation with his wife and children.

Better Safe Than Sorry

Although the need for a practical polio vaccine was urgent—thousands of people were dying of polio every year—in early 1953 Salk was concerned about the risks of moving too fast with his experimental vaccine, and he worried that others might exaggerate his progress. In the *Journal of the American Medical Association*, Salk wrote:

"Although the results obtained in these studies can be regarded as encouraging, they should *not* be interpreted to indicate that a practical vaccine is now at hand. . . . It will now be necessary to establish precisely the limits within which the effects here described can be reproduced with certainty.

"Because of the great importance of safety factors in studies of this kind, it must be remembered that considerable time is required for the preparation and study of each new batch of experimental vaccine before human **inoculations** can be considered. It is this consideration, above all else, that imposes a limitation on the speed with which this work can be extended."

CHAPTER 6 | TRIUMPH

After Salk's experimental vaccine became public knowledge in early 1953, pressure mounted to speed up the development efforts. Salk was reluctant to commit himself to a precise date for when the vaccine would be ready for large-scale testing in a field trial, but he finally agreed that late 1953 or early 1954 was a possibility. The trial had to begin before summer, when the polio season began. Once the season was under way, researchers would not be able to tell if a polio case had occurred because the person had become infected before being vaccinated, or because the vaccine simply wasn't working.

The field trial was organized by the National Foundation for Infantile Paralysis, which also paid its costs. To ensure that the findings would be objective and impartial, the foundation decided that the trial should be supervised by a separate group, which would analyze the data. Thomas Francis of the University of Michigan agreed to take on this assignment. The field trial began in late April 1954. It was preceded by a smaller, preliminary test conducted by Salk on a few thousand Pittsburgh schoolchildren.

Mary Kosloski, the 1955 March of Dimes poster child, and Randy Kerr, the first "Polio Pioneer."

POLIO PIONEERS

The very first of the "Polio Pioneers"—as the children who took part in the trial were called—was six-year-old Randy Kerr of Fairfax County, Virginia. Kerr received his shot and his Polio Pioneer button at 9 a.m. on April 26, 1954.

Test or No Test?

Until the very start of the field trial, a sharp debate raged among polio experts as to whether it should be given the green light. Albert Sabin criticized the trial in testimony before the U.S. Congress, and he warned Salk that the vaccine was "potentially unsafe" and would destroy his career. The well-known radio and television broadcaster and newspaper columnist Walter Winchell caused a stir in early April when he reported the Salk vaccine "may be a killer." He said it had killed several monkeys, and he claimed that the National Foundation for Infantile Paralysis was stockpiling "little white coffins" in preparation for the trial. The foundation refuted the untrue allegations, but Winchell's story did result in some people dropping out of the trial.

Broadcaster and newspaper columnist Walter Winchell

More than 1.8 million children ultimately took part in the trial. They were divided into three groups. One group received the vaccine, while another group received a harmless **placebo**. The trial was a "double-blind"—neither the children nor the persons administering the vaccination knew whether any given shot contained vaccine or a placebo. A double-blind trial guaranteed the fairest and most objective study possible. The third group of children received neither vaccine nor placebo. They were so-called "observation controls"—researchers monitored their health for comparison to the other two groups.

In addition to the children taking part in the trial, hundreds of thousands of adults were also involved. Most of the people who helped carry out the trial were volunteers. They numbered more than 200,000, and many of them belonged to local chapters of the National Foundation for Infantile Paralysis. Professionals who took part in the trial included 20,000 doctors, 40,000

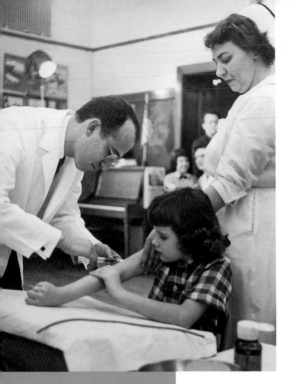

Salk gives a shot to a Pittsburgh girl during the 1954 field trial of the polio vaccine.

nurses, 50,000 schoolteachers, and 14,000 school principals. The trial dominated the headlines. A May 1954 Gallup poll found that nine out of every ten Americans knew about the trial—more than could give the full name of the country's president (Dwight David Eisenhower).

FRANCIS REPORT

Francis and his staff did not have computers, so they spent months compiling and evaluating the data from the trial. He reported the results at the University of Michigan in Ann Arbor on April 12, 1955—which, by coincidence, was the tenth anniversary of Franklin Roosevelt's death. Salk's vaccine, Francis said, was "safe, effective and potent." According to the trial, the vaccination was 60 to 70 percent effective against paralysis caused by the Type I polio virus, more than 90 percent effective against Type II and Type III, and 94 percent effective against a severe form of the disease known as bulbar poliomyelitis.

Five hundred noted doctors and scientists came to see Francis make his report, Salk among them. Some 150 reporters and commentators also attended, and the event, which was broadcast on radio and television, turned into a media circus. One of the journalists who described the scene commented, "Newsmen were jumping over each other and screaming, 'It works! It works!'" *The New York Times* reported, "The formal verdict on the Salk vaccine was disclosed today amid fanfare and drama far more typical of a Hollywood premiere than a medical meeting." This hullabaloo disgusted some of the scientists who attended. "The bedlam was revolting," one said. "It

Salk versus Sabin

Among Salk's critics, one of the most outspoken was Albert Sabin, Salk's chief competitor in the effort to develop a polio vaccine. The two scientists feuded for years. Each was a strong-minded person who firmly believed that his position was correct. Sabin favored the traditional live-virus approach to creating a vaccine, while Salk pursued the then-unconventional killed-virus approach.

Personality differences also played a role in the conflict. The two men simply did not get along. Sabin was already an expert researcher in the polio field when Salk began working on a polio vaccine, and the older Sabin seems to have viewed Salk as an upstart. Salk never forgot an early incident that took place during a meeting in connection with the polio typing project. Seeking to introduce a new approach, Salk asked a question. As Salk later recalled, "Albert Sabin sat back and turned to me and said, 'Now, Dr. Salk, you should know better than to ask a question like that.' It was like being kicked in the teeth. I had offered an oblique challenge to one of the assumptions, you see, and now I was being put in my place. I could feel the resistance and the hostility and the disapproval. I never attended a single one of those meetings afterward without that same feeling."

Later, Salk's quick progress with his vaccine seemed to irritate Sabin, whose work on a live-virus vaccine was proceeding more slowly—in part, he suspected, because Salk's killed-virus program was drawing research grants that could have been applied instead to the live-virus effort. Sabin did, however, make an important contribution to the development of Salk's vaccine. By pointing out the vaccine's potential drawbacks or defects, Sabin helped ensure that the field trial of 1954 was done as carefully and safely as possible.

was as if four supermarkets were having their premieres on the same day in the same parking lot."

A SCIENTIST BECOMES A STAR

After Francis's announcement, a wave of excitement swept across the country. Church bells rang, fire sirens sounded, and resolutions were issued honoring Salk. To the public, Salk seemed a wonderfully appealing figure, not at all like the stereotype of the stuffy old scientist. He was just forty years old, a young miracle worker with an appealing smile and an attractive family. Salk also did not seem at all eager to profit from his vaccine. He turned down a Hollywood offer to make a movie about his life, starring Marlon Brando. During a television interview, the well-known journalist and broadcaster Edward R. Murrow asked Salk who owned the patent on the vaccine. Salk replied, "Well the people, I would say. There is no patent. Could you patent the sun?" (Actually, patents and royalties were not allowed under the terms of the grants that were given out by the National Foundation for Infantile Paralysis.)

In that same interview, Murrow warned Salk about the changes that awaited him. "Young man," Murrow said, "a great tragedy has just befallen you." Salk asked, "What's that, Ed?" Murrow replied, "You've just lost your **anonymity**." Murrow was correct. At the guesthouse in Ann Arbor where the Salk family stayed when Francis made his announcement, Salk was deluged with phone calls and telegrams. Salk hadn't expected to turn into a world-famous celebrity. He just wanted to "get back to the laboratory," but, as Morrow had pointed out, life would never again be the same for him.

After the Salks returned to Pittsburgh, the public adoration continued. Salk received a telegram signed by more than seven thousand people in Winnipeg, Canada. It was 208 feet (63 meters) long. Salk was even called to the White House on April 22 to receive a special citation from President Eisenhower. Once, when Salk's son Peter heard the name "Salk" on the car radio, he said, "Dad, I'd rather be an ordinary person like me than famous and bothered like you."

In 1960, Salk and U.S president Dwight Eisenhower celebrate the fifth anniversary of the introduction of the Salk polio vaccine.

VACCINE PRODUCTION

The same day Francis announced the results of the field trial, Oveta Culp Hobby, the U.S. Secretary of Health, Education, and Welfare, signed the papers permitting commercial production of the Salk vaccine. The vaccination of children began quickly, because the National Foundation for Infantile Paralysis, wanting to be ready if the Francis report was positive, had already arranged for drug manufacturers to produce large supplies of the vaccine. The foundation sought to vaccinate as many children as possible before the polio season started.

A couple of weeks after vaccinations began, however, they were suddenly halted when several children who received shots developed polio. A total of more than two hundred cases of polio, with eleven cases resulting in death, were reported. It turned out that Cutter Laboratories, one of the vaccine manufacturers, had failed to follow Salk's instructions precisely, and not all the viruses in its vaccine were killed. Once the problem was found and vaccine supplies were checked, the vaccinations continued.

San Diego school-children line up for polio vaccine shots in April 1955.

Salk (right) and a research assistant check test tubes in 1955.

CHAPTER 7

AFTER THE VACCINE

On April 12, 1955, the day Francis reported the success of the Salk vaccine, Salk had breakfast with Alan Gregg, the vice president of the Rockefeller Foundation (an organization that funded medical research). Francis stopped by and told the two men that his report on the field trials would be positive. Gregg asked Salk what he planned to do next. Salk replied that there were some polio questions he still wanted to study, and that his university wanted him to head a new department of microbiology and preventive medicine. Apart from these goals, however, he wasn't sure about his future. "Jonas," Gregg advised, "do only that which makes your heart leap." Salk eventually decided to establish a new institute where talented specialists in science and the arts could work together to explore the basic principles of life and the human mind.

SALK INSTITUTE FOR BIOLOGICAL STUDIES

Salk (left) in his
Pittsburgh lab
in 1962

Basil O'Connor, the head of the National Foundation for Infantile Paralysis, supported Salk's vision for a new institute, and the foundation provided money to get the project started. The Salk Institute was incorporated in 1960. Salk and O'Connor selected a picturesque site on the Pacific Ocean in La Jolla, California, outside of San Diego. A famous architect, Louis Kahn, designed the institute's buildings, but Salk took an active part in the process, and the remarkable structures that were built won several architectural honors. The first laboratories were opened in 1963, although construction was not yet completed. Salk became the institute's first director.

Global Eradication of Polio

In 1988, an estimated 350,000 new cases of polio occurred in 125 countries. That year, the World Health Organization (WHO) began a vaccination campaign aimed at eliminating polio around the world by 2000. Although this goal was not met, considerable progress has been made in wiping out the disease. In 2002, fewer than 2,000 polio cases were reported in seven countries. The WHO hopes polio will be completely eradicated before the end of the decade.

In 1994, North and South America were certified as being almost completely free of the polio virus, except for a very few cases caused by the Sabin vaccine or by viruses that were brought in from other parts of the world. In 2000, countries in the western Pacific region were declared similarly polio-free, followed by Europe and central Asia in 2002.

A WHO worker gives the Sabin oral polio vaccine to a child in Somalia, a country in Africa.

Salk with his second wife, Françoise Gilot

The Salk Institute never really achieved Salk's dream of mixing prominent biological scientists with leaders in other disciplines. It did, however, become a major center for biological research, focusing on such areas as molecular biology, genetics, the neurosciences, and plant biology.

As Salk built his institute, his marriage was failing. Donna Salk did not enjoy her husband's new celebrity, and she did not like the entertaining and the social appearances that came with Salk's fund-raising and administrative work. The couple divorced in 1968. Two years later, Salk married Fançoise Gilot, a French painter who had once been the companion of the famous artist Pablo Picasso.

Recognition Denied?

Salk received quite a few honors for his work, including the Congressional Gold Medal in 1955 and the Presidential Medal of Freedom in 1977. In 1956, he won the Albert Lasker Award for Clinical Research, which is one of the most prestigious honors in medical science. He was named a Chevalier of the French Legion of Honor.

But Salk failed to win the Nobel Prize and he was never selected for membership in the U.S. National Academy of Sciences. Very few scientists win the Nobel Prize, and the fact that Enders, Weller, and Robbins earned a Nobel for polio-related research may have made it harder for Salk to have a chance. But Salk had also provoked resentment among other scientists. Many accused him of being too aggressive, too self-confident, and too hungry for personal fame, and they disliked the media circus that had unfolded when Thomas Francis gave his report about the Salk vaccine field trials. Some scientists also claimed that, while Salk was a good research team manager and made some technical improvements in research techniques, he was not a truly creative thinker. "Salk was strictly a kitchen chemist," his longtime rival Albert Sabin reportedly said. "He never had an original idea in his life." In addition, some of Salk's fellow researchers apparently were jealous of the generous funding he received from the National Foundation for Infantile Paralysis, the president of which, Basil O'Connor, Salk counted as a good friend.

Once Salk settled in at the institute, he found time to do some research. He worked on such diseases as cancer, multiple sclerosis, and, in the final years of his life, AIDS. He also wrote several books, which were more philosophical than scientific, on science, social problems, and other topics. Salk died of congestive heart failure on June 23, 1995, in La Jolla. He was eighty years old, but he had never stopped asking questions about the world around him.

Salk in his office at the Salk Institute, 1980

TIMELINE

1914	Jonas Salk is born on October 28 in New York City
1916	United States suffers its first major polio epidemic
1918	Influenza epidemic kills millions of people around the world
1921	Future U.S. president Franklin Delano Roosevelt is diagnosed with polio
1934	Salk graduates from college with a bachelor of science degree. Enters the New York University School of Medicine
1938	The National Foundation for Infantile Paralysis is established
1939	Salk graduates from medical school, marries Donna Lindsay
1940	Becomes an intern at Mount Sinai Hospital in New York
1942	Moves to the University of Michigan, where he works under Thomas Francis on influenza vaccines
1947	Moves to the University of Pittsburgh, where he runs his own lab and begins working on the polio virus
1948	Salk and other researchers begin major effort to identify types of polio viruses. (In 1949, scientists discover a way to produce large amounts of the polio virus for study related to developing a vaccine.)
1950	Salk starts working on a polio vaccine using killed viruses
1952	The United States reports almost 58,000 new cases of polio. Salk tests his polio vaccine on small numbers of people
1954	Huge field trial of Salk's vaccine, involving more than 1.8 million children, is carried out across the United States
1955	Salk's vaccine is found to be safe and effective. The U.S. government authorizes commercial production of the vaccine
1957	Less than 5,500 new polio cases are reported in the United States
1963	The Salk Institute for Biological Studies opens, with Salk as its first director
1977	Receives the Presidential Medal of Freedom
1995	Dies on June 23 of congestive heart failure

TRAILBLAZERS
of the MODERN WORLD

JONAS
SALK

WORLD ALMANAC®
LIBRARY

GLOSSARY

anonymity: the state of being anonymous.

antibodies: special proteins produced by the body's immune system to defend against foreign substances or organisms, such as viruses or bacteria.

anti-Semitism: hostility toward Jews.

biochemistry: the study of the chemicals and chemical processes in organisms.

epidemic: the widespread outbreak of a disease.

epidemiologist: a scientist who studies the spread and control of diseases.

field trial: a test of something experimental, such as a vaccine, in the way in which it will actually be used.

formaldehyde: a chemical that is often used to kill infectious microorganisms.

Great Depression: a severe economic slump in the United States and other countries that persisted throughout the 1930s.

immune system: the body's system for defending against foreign substances or organisms that may cause disease.

inoculation: the introduction of a vaccine or other substance into the body to stimulate the production of antibodies.

iron lung: a large machine once used to help polio patients with paralyzed lung muscles. Enclosing almost the entire body, it helped patients breathe by forcing air in and out of their lungs.

microorganisms: very tiny organisms that can only be seen with a microscope.

newsreels: short films featuring news of the day. In the 1930s, newsreels were shown before the start of a movie.

placebo: a substitute for a drug or vaccine having no effect upon a person.

pre-med: college courses that help prepare a person for medical school.

quarantined: isolated from other people.

smallpox: a contagious and often fatal disease that causes fever and skin rashes.

ultraviolet light: energy in the form of light that cannot be seen by the human eye.

vaccine: a substance introduced into the body to cause immunity to a disease.

TO FIND OUT MORE

BOOKS

Bankston, John. *Jonas Salk and the Polio Vaccine (Unlocking the Secrets of Science).* Bear, Delaware: Mitchell Lane, 2002.

Barter, James. *The Importance of Jonas Salk (Importance of).* San Diego: Lucent, 2002.

Durrett, Deanne. *Jonas Salk (Inventors and Creators).* San Diego: Kidhaven Press, 2002.

McPherson, Stephanie Sammartino. *Jonas Salk: Conquering Polio (Lerner Biographies).* Minneapolis: Lerner, 2002.

Naden, Corinne J., and Rose Blue. *Jonas Salk: Polio Pioneer.* Brookfield, Conn.: Millbrook Press, 2001.

Seavey, Nina Gilden, Jane S. Smith, and Paul Wagner. *A Paralyzing Fear: The Triumph Over Polio in America.* New York: TV Books, 1998.

Tocci, Salvatore. *Jonas Salk: Creator of the Polio Vaccine (Great Minds of Science).* Berkeley Heights, N. J.: Enslow Publishers, 2003.

INTERNET SITES

End of Polio
http://www.endofpolio.org/
Pictures and commentary on the history of polio and on the global effort to eliminate the disease.

Franklin & Eleanor Roosevelt Institute: FDR and Polio
http://www.feri.org/archives/polio
Information about U.S. president Franklin D. Roosevelt's experiences with polio.

Polio History Pages
http://www.cloudnet.com/~edrbsass/poliohistorypage.htm
Information about polio and its history, including excerpts from interviews with people who survived the disease.

Science Odyssey: People and Discoveries — Jonas Salk 1914–1995
http://www.pbs.org/wgbh/aso/databank/entries/bmsalk.html
Biographical information about Jonas Salk, with links to information on the development of the polio vaccine and a comic-strip style presentation of the polio virus and its crippling effects.

INDEX

About the Author

Richard Hantula has written and edited books and articles on science, medicine, and health for more than two decades. He was the senior U.S. editor for the Macmillan Encyclopedia of Science. Born in Michigan, he has lived in New York City since the late 1970s.

TRAILBLAZERS of the MODERN WORLD

Modern history is filled with stories of people whose lives have changed the world. Some excelled in sports and transformed our ideas of what athletes can achieve. Others made scientific or technical contributions that touched the lives of all who came after them. Still others were political and social leaders who changed the way we view the world.

The *Trailblazers of the Modern World* series closely examines the lives of such people—showing what challenges they faced, how they attained their fame, and why we are better today for their efforts.

Engaging prose, selections from primary source documents, and enlightening illustrations, including historic photos, help the reader understand the magnitude of these trailblazers. Each book includes a timeline, a glossary, a list of books and Web sites for more information, and an index.

JONAS SALK

One such trailblazer is Jonas Salk, an American physician who developed the first vaccine for poliomyelitis, or polio, in the 1950s. Before Salk developed his vaccine, many people lived in fear of polio, an infectious disease that mostly affects children and can cause paralysis. Today, thanks to the widespread use of polio vaccines, polio has largely disappeared from many parts of the world.

 WORLD ALMANAC® LIBRARY

ISBN 0-8368-5260-5

9 780836 852608